Arabian
Horses

ABDO
Publishing Company

A Buddy Book
by
Julie Murray

VISIT US AT
www.abdopub.com

Published by Buddy Books, an imprint of ABDO Publishing Company, 4940 Viking Drive, Suite 622, Edina, Minnesota 55435. Copyright © 2003 by Abdo Consulting Group, Inc. International copyrights reserved in all countries. No part of this book may be reproduced in any form without written permission from the publisher.

Printed in the United States.

Edited by: Christy DeVillier
Contributing Editors: Matt Ray, Michael P. Goecke
Graphic Design: Maria Hosley
Image Research: Deborah Coldiron
Cover Photograph: Corel
Photographs: Corel, Photodisc

Library of Congress Cataloging-in-Publication Data

Murray, Julie, 1969-
   Arabian horses/Julie Murray.
      p. cm. — (Animal kingdom)
   Includes bibliographical references (p.).
   Summary: An introduction to the history, physical characteristics, and behavior of the Arabian horse, the oldest horse breed in the world.
   ISBN 1-57765-701-2
      1. Arabian horse—Juvenile literature. [1.Arabian horse. 2. Horses.] I. Title.

SF293.A8 M87 2002
636.1'12—dc21

2001058982

Contents

Horses

Horses have been helping people for thousands of years. Before trains, horses were the fastest way of traveling. No other animal could pull or carry people so quickly. Today, many people get around using cars, bikes, or buses. Yet, people still love riding horses for fun.

Over the years, people have used horses for many things.

Arabian Horses

Arabian horses are famous for their grace, beauty, and speed. These horses have been around for more than 5,000 years. In fact, the Arabian horse is the oldest breed in the world. The first Arabian horses probably lived in the Middle East.

Arabian Horses Today

People use Arabian horses for racing and long-distance riding. Many people train their Arabians for horse shows, too. Just being near these beautiful animals is enough for some people. Spending time with horses can be fun.

Color And Size

The first Arabian horses may have been bay or chestnut colored. A bay-colored horse is reddish-brown. It also has a black mane, black legs, and a black tail. Chestnut-colored horses are golden-brown. Today, Arabian horses may be gray or black, too.

Arabian horses can be many colors.

People measure horses in hands.
One hand equals four inches (10 cm).
Arabian horses stand about 14 to 15
hands tall to their shoulders. This is
about five feet (1.5 m) tall. They weigh
between 800 and 1,000 pounds (363
and 454 kg). The Arabian horse is
smaller than most other breeds.

Arabian
14-15 hands

Thoroughbred
15-17 hands

This young Arabian horse has bay coloring.

Head And Body

The Arabian horse's head is shorter than some other breeds. It has large nostrils and large, wide-set eyes. A small dip below the eyes gives the Arabian a "dished" face. Its mane and tail are full of soft, thin hair.

Arabian horses have big nostrils and wide-set eyes.

Arabian horses have 17 ribs. Other horses have 18 ribs. The Arabian horse's lower back has five vertebrae. Other horses have six vertebrae in their lower back. These differences give Arabian horses a special body shape.

Eating

Horses use their back teeth for chewing. They use their front teeth for biting. Horses need about 15 pounds (7 kg) of food every day. Arabian horses eat grass, hay, oats, and bran. Horses need water each day, too.

Arabian horses eating grass.

Understanding Horses

Horses do not like to be alone. In the wild, they live together in herds. Smelling and touching one another helps horses to bond. Friendship can happen when horses groom each other.

Horses like to be around each other.

The best way to bond with a horse is to spend time with it.

Horses also bond with people. Horses learn their owner's voice. They learn their owner's smell, too. Through smell, horses know if their owner is nervous or afraid. A horse that trusts its owner can become a special friend.

Foals

Female horses, or mares, can have a baby once a year. A baby horse is called a foal. Wild mares usually have their foals in the spring.

Mares have one foal at a time.

Newborn foals can stand within minutes. They will drink their mother's milk for about six months. Six-week-old foals will begin to eat other food. Horses become full grown after five or six years. Horses may live for 25 years.

A young foal stays close to its mother.

Important Words

breed a special group of horses. Horses of the same breed look alike and share some strengths.

groom to clean and care for. Removing insect pests is one way horses groom each other.

hand something used to measure horses. One hand equals four inches (10 cm).

mane the longer hair that grows on a horse's neck and back.

nostrils the openings or holes of a nose.

vertebrae parts that make up an animal's backbone, or spine.

Web Sites

Arabian Home Page

www.imh.org/imh/bw/arabian.html
Learn more about Arabian horses and discover organizations that promote this breed.

My Horse.com

www.myhorse.com
A special section for young riders offers horse tips, articles, and games. A searchable list of horse events is also featured at this site.

Horsefun

http://horsefun.com
This site is made for kids who love horses.
It features games, puzzles, and a quiz.

Index